Understanding, receiving and embracing

The Life
God Wants
to Give You

Patty,
May you experience
the fulness of
every blessing God
has
for you!

Bruce Byrne

© Bruce Byrne 2012

ISBN 978-1-300-23825-6

Quotes from the Bible are from
the New International Version

Dedication

To my wife, Melinda, who
always encourages and always believes.

Foreword

In the summer of 1988, I accepted a call to pastor a small Presbyterian congregation in Concord, California, inheriting a staff which included Bruce Byrne as my part-time Director of Youth Ministry. We quickly became friends and I soon began to appreciate the teaching abilities of my new partner in ministry.

You'll discover, through this book, what I've known for years—Bruce has a gift for communicating the gospel with clarity. For over twenty years, I've watched Bruce make the essentials of the Christian faith accessible to middle schoolers and I've seen him engaging adults with a substance and style that blesses even committed veterans of the faith with new insight and understanding.

I'm excited for the impact this book will have on my parishioners and I look forward to preaching within its structure, but I'm even more excited about the impact it will have on those for whom the gospel is an unfamiliar story. Through these pages, I'm convinced that many will come to understand, receive and embrace the life God wants to give them.

Daniel Vraa, Pastor
Dixon Community Church
Dixon, California

Table of Contents

Preface

Early in my youth ministry career, while I was wrapping up a lesson and short on time, a young man asked a profound question. Recognizing its importance, but also knowing that I couldn't adequately address it given the time constraints, I promised to devote the next week's lesson to the answer.

During the next week I put considerable thought and energy into my lesson preparation and by the time our next meeting rolled around I was ready. The young man who had asked the question, however, was a no show.

Anyone who has ever taught within a youth ministry context will have had a similar experience. There will be times when you prepare a lesson everyone needs to hear and only a few show up. What then? Those who weren't there need to be exposed to the content, but you can't repeat the same lesson the next week without losing the interest of those who've already heard it.

This is also the case for the pastor who preaches to the same flock week after week, year after year. How do you make sure people are exposed to and understand the essentials while avoiding a reputation for repetitiveness?

Of course, this assumes that the essentials are being communicated at all. At the time of this writing, I've been blessed to have been teaching young people in a youth ministry context for over thirty years. Looking back, I recognize that the content of my lessons in the early days was heavily weighted toward my own interests and needs and that my own understanding was often lacking. I've had occasion to wonder if, back in those early days, I was able to effectively communicate the essentials to those in my care, even to those who attended regularly.

Thus the original motivation behind this small book: To put in one place a concise treatment of that which matters most. For those who knew me from the earliest days, this is what I should have been teaching you, and to those from the latter days, this is what you would have heard if you had attended regularly.

Although the group for whom I originally intended this work was relatively small, I'd be delighted, of course, if it found a wider audience. It is my prayer that those who already possess the gifts of God will come through these words to a deeper understanding and appreciation for what they have been given. And for those for whom these words serve as an introduction, it is my prayer that they will come to possess and enjoy forever the life God wants to give them.

Chapter

1

Just Six Things

Imagine that you're a homeless person living on the streets. You spend your days begging for money and collecting aluminum cans. On a good day your efforts provide you with enough income for two, maybe three meals. Hunger is a constant companion.

But your life takes a sudden turn for the better when, early one morning, a limousine pulls up to the curb near where you've been sleeping and a man gets out and approaches you. He asks you a few questions and, once satisfied with your answers, identifies himself as the manager of your great Aunt Gracie's estate and informs you of the news: Your great Aunt Gracie has died and left her estate to you. Though somewhat groggy, you accept the man's offer to drive you to your new home. On the way, he explains:

"Upon the death of your parents some seven years ago, your great aunt rewrote her will to recognize that you were now her sole heir. Two months ago, when it was learned that you were living on the streets, she authorized me to determine your needs and to change her will accordingly. Not knowing the details of how you came to be in your current situation, it was decided that it would be unwise to simply grant you control of the estate. Rather, a trust was set up which will more than provide for your needs for the rest of your life. The trust administrators are tasked with managing the upkeep of your estate, providing for your medical care and other necessities— food, clothing and the like. You will also be provided with spending money, some $2,500 a month. And, at your great aunt's insistence, my services are also covered as the Head of Staff to your security, kitchen and groundskeeping staffs." Twenty minutes later you arrive at your estate and begin a new life.

How has your life changed as a consequence of your inheritance? You're no longer homeless, of course. Where once you slept on the streets, you now enjoy the clean sheets of your own bed. Where you once had access only to the most basic medical care, you now have first class treatment. Where you had to scrounge and beg for food, you now have a kitchen staff to prepare warm, nutritious meals for you. You have spending money. You have security. Everything has changed for the better.

Of course, there will be challenges ahead. No longer living in survival mode, you'll have free time to either waste or spend productively. You'll have to grapple with your own identity and sense of purpose. There will be moments when you wake up in the middle of the night wondering which back alleyway you're sleeping in. But there's no question that, as a result of your Aunt Gracie's generosity, your life has been completely changed for the better.

But consider a different ending to the story: What if all the details of the inheritance were the same, but no one ever showed up to tell you about it? How would your life change if the inheritance existed, but you weren't aware of it? The answer, of course, is that your life wouldn't be any different. Despite owning an estate, you'd still be living on the streets. Despite having an entire kitchen staff at your disposal, you'd still be scrounging for your next meal. Ironically, your own security staff could unwittingly keep you from begging for a meal at the door of your own home.

Consider yet another possibility: All the details of the inheritance are the same as above, but, somehow, you're only made aware of one or two of the details. Let's say that you only hear about (and have access to) the $2,500 per month spending money. What then? How is your life impacted? Well, $2,500 a month is probably enough to provide you with food and some sort of shelter, so your life would be greatly impacted for the better, but it isn't much in comparison with the fullness of your inheritance. You'd probably be forever grateful to your aunt Gracie for her generosity, but if you only knew how much more was yours....

From an emotional perspective, imagine how it would feel to go from homelessness to the fullness of your inheritance. When it finally sunk in, when you finally realized that your life of poverty was over, when you first comprehended all that you now had, what would your response be? The cold, hungry nights are gone. The days spent begging are over. How would you feel?

But what would your emotional response be if you inherited your great aunt's estate but never got word of it? Obviously, without knowledge of the inheritance, you'd have no emotional response at all. The fear and anxiety that were a constant part of living on the streets would continue just as before.

And what of our third scenario, where you are only made aware of a part of your inheritance? I'm sure learning that you'd be receiving $2,500 every month for the rest of your life would be a cause of great relief, joy and gratitude, but, again, how much greater would your relief, joy and gratitude be if you knew the fullness of your inheritance?

The Bible teaches that there is an inheritance available to us—an inheritance from God every bit as life changing as the one described above. Some, like a homeless person who never gets word, live unaware of all that could be theirs. Others have heard of the inheritance and enjoy it, but only in part. Still others enjoy the inheritance for a time, but end up back in their old manner of living. Then there are those who understand, receive and embrace the inheritance gifts, and, consequently, live lives full of relief, joy and gratitude. This is the life God wants to give you. This is the life you were made for.

* * *

Before the homeless man in our story could enjoy his inheritance, the manager of aunt Gracie's estate had to show up and tell him about it. For over thirty years, it's been my privilege to serve in a role that is similar to aunt Gracie's manager. As a Director of Youth Ministry, it's been my responsibility to teach young people about the inheritance God has for them.

If you haven't heard about or have an incomplete understanding of what the Bible teaches about the life God wants to give you, this book was written with you in mind—that you may come to understand, receive and fully embrace it. For this to happen, it's necessary to understand just six things (then a seventh) and, in the chapters ahead, we'll look at each in turn.

The limo is at the curb. The door is open. If you'll come along with me, I'll share with you the six then seven things you need to know in order to understand, receive and embrace the life you were made for.

For a number of reasons, I've chosen to begin (in the next chapter) with a brief introduction to the second thing. After the next chapter, we'll backtrack to the first thing and then proceed in order.

Chapter

2

The Second Thing:
God's Response to Our Need
(Part One)

The Gift Package

Every good and perfect gift is from above...

A wealthy surgeon, having lost his wife and son in a car accident, decides that he needs a break from the routine of his life and offers his services to a hospital in Port-au-Prince, Haiti free of charge for one year. At the end of his fourth month, as he is walking back to the hospital after a lunch break, he happens upon a malnourished orphan boy lying in a muddy alleyway. The boy is alive, but in desperate shape. As the doctor examines him, he discovers that the boy has a heart defect, something that will take his life—unless he has immediate surgery. After carrying the boy to the hospital, the doctor quickly prepares to perform the surgery and, having done so, arranges for the boy's extensive recuperation.

Six month later, after a long and difficult recovery, the boy is ready to be discharged from the hospital and the doctor faces a dilemma: He has saved the boy's life, but has he saved it only to have him return to a life of homelessness, poverty and hunger? Of course this is unacceptable, and with only a couple of months of his stay in Haiti left, the doctor quickly makes plans to see that all of the boy's needs will be met. In addition to ongoing medical treatment, the boy will need shelter, clothing and food. He'll also need to be educated so that he will eventually be able to support himself. And he'll need some spending money—not necessarily a lot, but just enough to meet unexpected needs and for an occasional treat. Most importantly, he'll need someone to watch over him, to supervise his continuing care, to assure that the doctor's wishes are carried out and to see that no one takes advantage of him. But who can he trust with such an important task?

Then one night, the doctor dreamt of the family he lost and, upon awakening, felt the pain of his loss as deeply as ever. Suddenly he knew what he most wanted: He wanted a family again, and in that moment he decided to adopt the boy. He would not only oversee his care, he would personally care for him, a father for a son.

* * *

In the first chapter, we considered the homeless man who was saved from homelessness by way of an inheritance. In this chapter, we read of an orphan child saved from illness and poverty through the kindness of a doctor. These are salvation stories, stories which relate the details of how someone in need comes to have their needs met.

Most of our stories, whether found in the books we read to children or in what we watch on television, are salvation stories: Someone needs saving and someone comes to save them. The saving might come by way of a kiss from a handsome prince, by the quick draw of a sheriff or by an ordinary person who puts their life at risk for the sake of someone else. In our story of the orphan boy, we encountered someone who had a variety of needs and who therefore needed saving in a variety of ways—no one thing could accomplish the saving on its own. The doctor, the savior in our story, recognized that the one time gift of surgery was not enough in itself to bring the boy to a life of health and wholeness. For that to be accomplished, a variety of ongoing gifts would be needed: Gifts of food, shelter, clothing and education, for example, would all have to be provided, and it is this gift package that saves the boy from a life of poverty and to the fullness of life the doctor desired for him.

Like the orphan in our story, our needs before God are many and varied. And like the doctor, God has put together a gift package—each gift designed to meet a specific need. Working together, the gifts of God meet our needs and accomplish the fullness of the salvation God wants us to have and enjoy.

Some of gifts in the salvation gift package have names that may be unfamiliar to you, and some may sound old fashioned or religious. We'll unwrap each gift in chapter four and I'll explain and define each of them for you, so don't let your unfamiliarity with them be of concern. For now, just know that the salvation God has for us includes:

- Forgiveness
- Justification
- Redemption
- Adoption
- Spiritual rebirth
- The giving of the Holy Spirit to live in and through us, to comfort us, to mature us, to guide us into truth, to pray with and for us, to give us gifts to use for his kingdom's sake and to remind us that we are God's children.
- Eternal life

These gifts make possible the fullness of life God desires us to have and enjoy. When we understand our needs and the thoroughness with which God has met them, we cannot help but respond in joy and gratitude.

*   *   *

     Thinking of what God has done for us in terms of a gift package can do a number of things for us. Most importantly, it can help us understand, appreciate and enjoy all that God has for us. But it should also help us make sense of "salvation language"—language which refers to salvation in whole or in part. Salvation is an extravagant gift comprised of many diverse and extravagant gifts. The result is a salvation language which is equally diverse and extravagant—and often bewildering to those who are unfamiliar with it. Understanding the key components of the gift package will help those who are unfamiliar with salvation language make sense of the conversation.

The First Thing:
Our Need

(What's the problem?)

Chapter
3

The First Thing:
Our Need

*...all have sinned
and fall short of the glory of God...*

Because the salvation gift package God offers us is designed to meet our needs, it's not possible to fully understand and enjoy what God has done for us without recognizing and understanding the nature of those needs. But recognizing and understanding our needs can be anything but straightforward.

A woman with a lump in her breast needs to be quickly diagnosed and then treated appropriately. An alcoholic needs to stop drinking. A girl with anorexia needs an accurate body image and adequate nutrition. A woman who has contracted a sexually transmitted disease needs medical treatment. A man with dementia, as his ability to reason deteriorates, needs specialized care. Yet the woman with the lump in her breast may avoid diagnosis out of fear. The alcoholic may deny that his drinking is a problem even after losing his job, home and family. The girl with anorexia may continue to see herself as fat even as she starves to death. The woman with the sexually transmitted disease may be too embarrassed to go see her doctor, and the man with dementia, unable to recognize that he can no longer care for himself, may resist those who are trying to help.

A whole host of defense mechanisms can interfere with our ability to recognize and respond appropriately to our physical and psychological needs. The bleaker the potential diagnosis, the more likely we are to want to run from it. The more shameful the condition, the more likely it is that we will attempt to hide it from ourselves and others, and the more the condition affects our perception, the less likely we are to be able to recognize it.

As we turn to consider the biblical diagnosis of our spiritual condition, we should not be surprised to find within ourselves similar degrees of resistance, avoidance and denial, nor should we expect that, on our own, we are capable of grasping the full extent of our need. Like the woman with the lump in her breast, we are inclined to avoid the diagnosis. Like the alcoholic, we are inclined to deny that there is anything wrong with us. Like the anorexic, we suffer from a distorted self image, a distorted spiritual self image, even as we experience spiritual starvation. Like the woman with the sexually transmitted disease, we may be too embarrassed—or too proud—to seek treatment. And like the man with dementia, our condition itself interferes with our ability to accurately grasp the true nature of our need.

The biblical diagnosis is bleak: We are lost and without hope of finding our own way. We are broken, unable to heal ourselves. Worse, we are enemies of God, spiritually dead and destined for an eternity apart from the source of all love, joy, peace and goodness. Our nature is fallen, sinful and incapable of pleasing God.

It is almost too much to bear. Left to our own resources, perhaps it is too much to bear. But we are not left to our own resources: The one who brings this hard-to-bear diagnosis is the same one who, out of great love for us, provides the cure. To our brokenness, God comes as healer. Though we are sinful, God himself pays the penalty for our sin and offers forgiveness. To our spiritual deadness, God offers rebirth, new life. Though we are destined for an eternity apart from him, God prepares a place where we can be with him forever.

Our need runs deep, but God's provision runs deeper still and with this knowledge we can embrace the truth, unpleasant though it is, and turn to receive the salvation God so wants us to enjoy. Though we may desire to run from the bad news of our diagnosis, when we stop running, God is right there with love, generosity, care and cure.

*   *   *

The biblical diagnosis is bleak, but is it accurate? When we stand back and consider all of humanity, it's not hard to see the brokenness, and it's not hard to find clear examples of evil and sinfulness. But what of ourselves?

To say that we are broken or sinful, or to say that we have a fallen nature is not to say that we are as broken, sinful or fallen as we could possibly be. Having cancer doesn't mean that we are nothing but sickness. But cancer, like sinfulness, grows and spreads, and God will one day put an end to both.

If you don't know what to make of the biblical diagnosis, if you don't know how or if it applies to you, I have a suggestion —pray. Ask God to reveal the truth to you. Say to God: "God, show me the truth in this matter. Am I really as broken, fallen and sinful as the Bible teaches?" It is my experience that God answers prayers like these.

*   *   *

While it is human nature to avoid coming to terms with our need, some may find it particularly difficult. Those who were mistreated as children, for instance, may hear in the biblical diagnosis, echos of past abuse. The boy who could never do anything good enough to please his father may find it particularly painful to acknowledge that he is incapable of pleasing God on his own. The woman who was constantly shamed as a child may find it difficult to face up to her own sinfulness.

But the hard to hear words from God are not like the hard to hear words of an abuser. Unlike the abuser's words, God's words to us are true, spoken in love and with our healing in mind.

That said, if your response to the biblical diagnosis is more than normal range resistance—if you find yourself re-experiencing old trauma, for instance—let it go. An accurate understanding of our spiritual condition is of great value, but God's ability to heal and save does not depend upon our ability to fully grasp the nature of our need.

The First Thing:
Our Need

We are lost, separated from God, sinful, fallen and destined for an eternity apart from God.

The Second Thing:
God's Response to Our Need

Chapter

4

The Second Thing:
God's Response to Our Need
(Part Two)

The Salvation Gift Package Explored

...the gift of God is eternal life in Christ Jesus our Lord.

The salvation gift package is intended by God to meet our needs and then some. To say "and then some" may be the understatement of all time, for in the salvation gift package, God provides us with all we need to live an abundant life fully connected to him for all eternity. Having mentioned some of the components of the gift package previously, we'll now briefly explore them here. The Salvation Gift Package includes:

Forgiveness

Imagine laboring under a debt so large that you had no hope of ever paying it back. And imagine the freedom you'd feel upon being released from such a debt.

With the gift of forgiveness, God cancels our sin debt such that no record of our sin remains, completely setting us free from its burden.

Justification

The concept of justification is difficult to convey because the word as it is used today has little in common with how it was used in the Bible. That said, if God had a book, a ledger, within which he kept a record of our every sin, and if we think of every sin as a debt for which God will hold us accountable, forgiveness, as we have seen, can be likened to the cancelation of the sum total of our debt. But with justification, when we examine the ledger, we see that not only has our debt been forgiven, but that someone else's great wealth has been transfered into our account. Forgiveness cancels our debt; justification infuses our account with riches.

Monetary debt is, of course, just a metaphor. What we're really talking about in God's ledger is a record of our sin which we cannot undo. To be justified in the biblical sense is to have the record of our sin erased—and replaced with someone else's goodness. Those who have been justified by God, therefore, enjoy a new standing with God; the books are clean and there is nothing left in the record to condemn us.

Redemption

Redemption isn't the most common of English words, but it is occasionally used in popular culture in ways which provide insight into its biblical meaning.

If you were in need of a thousand dollars, you might take something of value (a wedding ring, for instance) to a pawn shop. If your item was worth more than a thousand dollars, the pawn shop owner would likely agree to give you the thousand dollars under the condition that if you returned within the month, you could *redeem* the ring for a thousand dollars plus the agreed upon interest. Until the month was up, the ring was still yours (it could not be sold to anyone else), but if you didn't return to redeem the ring, it would become the property of the pawn shop and it could then be sold.

When something is redeemed, two things are taking place: A right of ownership is asserted and a price is paid. In our redemption, God claims us as his own and pays the price that we might belong to him again.

Another way redemption is used in popular culture is in the context of someone making up for a mistake. A baseball player, for instance, who hits a three run homer after previously committing an error which allowed two runs to score is said to have "redeemed himself". In a biblical context, however, redemption comes not through our own actions, but by the actions of God.

Adoption

While we are all familiar with the concept of adoption, we ought not let such familiarity keep us from marveling at the scope of this great gift: God himself desires and offers to adopt us into his family.

In the Jewish culture of Jesus' day, there was no distinction made between an adopted child and a child who was born into the family and thus there was no second class or diminished status for the adopted. The same is true for those adopted into God's family.

It is common today for people to say, "We are all God's children," but this is contrary to what the Bible teaches. While we are all created in God's image (and thus have immeasurable value to God), only those who have received salvation are adopted into God's family. Only then is God truly our father and only then have we truly become God's children. (How the salvation gifts are received is the topic of chapters ten, eleven and twelve.)

Spiritual rebirth

When God forgives us, our sin is pardoned. When God justifies us, the record of our sin is erased and replaced with the record of Jesus' righteousness. When God redeems us, he claims us as his own. When God adopts us, we are welcomed into his family. Everything has changed except for one thing: We are still the same.

With spiritual rebirth, the change God makes is not to our circumstances or status, but to our spiritual nature—who we are at the core of our being. Our old spiritual nature, corrupted by sin and unable to please God, is done away with and a new nature, capable of doing and becoming everything God desires us to do and become, is given to us.

Those who have been spiritually reborn are born of God. They are members of God's family, not merely through the legal procedure of adoption, but by birth.

The giving of the Holy Spirit

The generosity of God doesn't stop with our spiritual rebirth. Additionally, God gives us his Holy Spirit to live in and through us, to comfort us, to help us to mature, to guide us into truth, to pray with and for us, to give us gifts to use for his kingdom's sake, to empower us and to testify to us that we are God's children.

Eternal life

The gifts of the salvation gift package are meant to be enjoyed for all eternity and God offers them to us lavishly and without end.

*   *   *

The above is just a brief look at the salvation God has made available to us, and each gift within the salvation gift package deserves much more attention than we can give it here.

In summary, God offers to us a salvation which meets our needs and then places us within the relationship he most desires to share with us: He invites us to be forgiven, justified, redeemed, adopted, spiritually reborn and filled with his Holy Spirit, and to enjoy this new relationship with him now and forever.

The First Thing:
Our Need

We are lost, separated from God, sinful, fallen, destined for an eternity apart from God.

The Second Thing:
God's Response to Our Need

The Salvation Gift Package

The Third Thing:
God's Motivation for Responding to Our Need

Chapter

5

The Third Thing:
God's Motivation for Responding
to Our Need

But because of his great love for us, God,
who is rich in mercy, made us alive with Christ...

Sometime during the autumn of my second grade year, as my friend and I were leaving the school grounds by the path which led out the back of the school yard, we saw a crowd gathering at the far edge of the field. Suspecting that a fight was about to break out, we quickened our pace and speculated as to who might be fighting. As we grew closer, we noticed that the crowd, roughly forming a semi-circle, was looking in our direction, back toward the school. Apparently they were waiting for someone. A few moments later I realized that it was me they were waiting for.

A girl, Angela, stepped toward me with a stick in her hand and fire in her eyes. Angela and I had a past. For a week or so during our first grade year, I had been smitten with Angela and had even visited her house on my way home from school once or twice. At her home I had been introduced to her dog and from that first introduction it wasn't clear who I was more smitten with, Angela or her dog. I loved that little beagle with all the affection my first grade heart could muster.

"How could you do that?" Angela asked, her voice controlled but fierce. I didn't know what she was talking about and told her so. She took another step in my direction and repeated her question.

Eventually the truth came out: Someone had told Angela that they had seen me trying to hurt her dog by poking it with a stick through the chain link fence that separated her backyard from the school yard. I don't remember the details of how our standoff ended, only that I was able to persuade her of my innocence. What I do remember is that look on her face. I didn't have a word for it then, I do now: It was wrath.

* * *

It may seem strange to begin a chapter on God's love with a story about wrath, but there is an intimate relationship between love and wrath that is often overlooked. Angela experienced wrath toward me because she believed I had tried to harm something she loved and wrath arises when someone intentionally harms (or attempts to harm) that which one loves — the greater the love, the greater the wrath.

It's not hard to step into Angela's shoes. As soon as we imagine someone being cruel to someone we love, wrath is right there with us. To say (as many do), "I believe in a God of love, not a God of wrath," is to misunderstand this fundamental truth. In a world where sin is rampant, where harm is intended, where injustice abounds, where people are used as a means to an end, the only possible way to have a God who isn't wrathful, is to have a God who doesn't love.

And God loves us dearly. He is wholly inclined to our wellbeing. He wants good things (and goodness itself) for us. He desires our health and wholeness. He values us beyond measure. We matter to him deeply. But out of God's love arises a dilemma.

Love desires the ultimate good for the one who is loved, whereas wrath finds its satisfaction in justice. If I had been guilty of taking a stick to Angela's dog, Angela would have been justified in taking a stick to me, and the stick in her hand would serve both as a means of protecting the good for the dog she loved and as a means of justice for the one toward whom she felt wrath. Because the object of her love and the object of her wrath were separate, both her love and her wrath could be expressed and satisfied.

But God's dilemma is this: There is no separation between those whom he loves and those toward whom he feels wrath—the objects of his love are also the objects of his wrath. As creatures made in God's image, we have immeasurable value to God, and as sinners, we have all stirred up God's wrath by harming those whom God loves. How then can both God's love and his wrath be satisfied?

In the salvation gift package, God offers to sinful humanity its ultimate good: Forgiveness, justification, redemption, adoption, rebirth, the indwelling of the Holy Spirit, eternal life (and more), and by it God's love for us is expressed and satisfied The extravagance of the salvation gift package provides us with a measure of God's love for us.

But it isn't until we understand the love/wrath dilemma and what God went through to resolve it for us so that we might become the recipients of his love (and only his love) that we can begin to grasp how "high and wide and long and deep" is the love God has for us. What God went through to resolve the love/ wrath dilemma in our favor is the subject of the next three chapters.

The First Thing:
Our Need

We are lost, separated from God, sinful, fallen, destined for an eternity apart from God.

The Second Thing:
God's Response to Our Need

The Salvation Gift Package

The Third Thing:
God's Motivation for Responding to Our Need

God responds to our need out of love, mercy and kindness

The Fourth Thing:
The Price God Paid for Our Salvation
(What It Cost God to Purchase Salvation for Us)

Chapter

6

The Fourth Thing:
The Price God Paid for Our Salvation
(Part One)

Keys and Fragments

This is how God showed his love among us:
He sent his one and only Son into the world...

Many years ago, my wife and I went to see a popular movie at our local multiplex. Running late, we hurried through the ticketing process, stopped to buy popcorn and drinks and then quickly walked down the long hallway until we found the individual theater in which our movie was playing. While we had hoped to miss only the previews, it was not to be—the movie had already started. We settled into our seats and began to take stock of the action.

Almost immediately I noticed that the characters on screen were having detailed conversations about things I knew nothing about. Then bullets began to fly, but it wasn't clear to me who was shooting at whom or which side I should be rooting for. I leaned over to my wife and whispered, "Is any of this making sense to you?" To my relief she said, "No." It was a few more minutes before we put the pieces together: The theater was showing this particular movie in two theaters and we had entered the wrong one. The movie we were watching was over half way through. Later, in the other theater, when we came to the part where we had originally entered, my wife leaned over to me and said, "It makes a lot more sense this time".

Some two thousand years ago a man was crucified by Roman soldiers on a hillside just outside the city of Jerusalem. While some celebrated and some mourned the death of Jesus of Nazareth, no one realized that the central event of human history had just unfolded. Jesus' death was not the result of unforeseen circumstances, nor was it a tragic ending to a man who inadvertently ended up in the middle of a political and religious conflict. It was part of the plan, God's plan for our salvation, from the beginning.

But understanding what Jesus accomplished on the cross and how the cross was part of the plan from the beginning is not possible without having at least some knowledge of salvation's back story—the history and context which led up to the cross and within which the cross makes sense.

In the next chapter, we'll rewind the movie of salvation to the beginning and then fast forward through it, pausing on several of the most significant scenes in salvation's back story. But first, in this chapter, I'll introduce five concepts and/or terms, some of which may seem of little importance at present, but which will later play key roles in shaping our understanding of salvation history.

The five concepts and/or terms are:

1) Representation and Identification

When Goliath stood in the valley facing the Israelites with the Philistine army behind him, he had a simple proposal: "Choose someone and send him out to fight me. If he wins, we will become your slaves, but if I win, you'll become ours". This challenge from Goliath went on for days without anyone volunteering to fight despite the king's promise of great reward for anyone who defeated him. Then a shepherd boy, while visiting his brothers who were serving in the army, heard the challenge and stepped forward. You probably know how the story ends: David felled Goliath with one stone from his sling. The Philistines, upon seeing their hero dead, turned and ran. All of Israel rejoiced in David's victory over Goliath and it's easy to understand why. Goliath represented the Philistine army which, in turn, represented the Philistine people. David represented the Israelite army which represented the Israelite people. Because David was identified with all of Israel, his victory was shared by all of Israel, just as Goliath's defeat was shared by all the Philistines.

Nations still send out armies to represent them in battle, but representation need not be as dramatic as in a military context. In a democracy, people elect representatives who act on their behalf, with the consequences, both great and small, being shared by all.

Representation can take many forms. As we've seen above, an individual can represent an individual or a group and a group can represent an individual or another group. Representation can be voluntary (as in a democracy) or involuntary (as with a court mandated attorney). Representation can be a matter of great consequence (as in a military campaign) or of a trivial nature (as in sporting events).

In the case of sporting events, people simply choose to identify themselves with a team and, having done so, share in "their" team's victories and losses.

2) Telestai

In New Testament times, when a bill or a debt had been paid off, the keeper of the record would write the Greek word

"Telestai" across its face. Telestai means, "paid in full".

3) The Temple Curtain

The temple in Jerusalem was arranged such that the deeper one progressed into it, the more sacred the space became. While even non-Jews were welcome in the outer court, only the priests were allowed into the Holy Place and only the High Priest was allowed into the Holy of Holies. Once a year, on the Day of Atonement, the High Priest went behind the curtain which separated the Holy of Holies from the Holy Place, entering, it was believed, into the very presence of God. The curtain which separated the Holy of Holies from the Holy Place was multilayered and has been described as being four to six inches thick.

4) Schizo

The Greek word "schizo" means "torn".

5) The Triune Nature of God

There is one God, but within God there exists three persons: The Father, the Son and the Holy Spirit. Each of these three persons is by nature God and each fully shares in all the attributes of God.

While understanding the nature of the Trinity may not be fully possible for human beings, Jesus' role in salvation cannot be understood without some familiarity with it.

For those who'd like to consider this aspect of God's nature more fully, please see the resources listed in the appendix.

The First Thing:
Our Need

We are lost, separated from God, sinful, fallen, destined for an eternity apart from God.

The Second Thing:
God's Response to Our Need

The Salvation Gift Package

The Third Thing:
God's Motivation for Responding to Our Need

God responds to our need out of love, mercy and kindness

The Fourth Thing:
The Price God Paid for Our Salvation
(What It Cost God to Purchase Salvation for Us)

Chapter

7

The Fourth Thing:
The Price God Paid for Our Salvation
(Part Two)

Salvation's Back Story

But when the set time had fully come,
God sent his Son... to redeem...

If we were to rewind God's plan of salvation to the beginning and then fast forward to the events most crucial to our understanding, it might look something like this:

The beginning

The Bible teaches that God created and that he was pleased with his creation. Soon after, however, humanity rebelled against God. Human nature became "fallen", marred by sin, broken. The human race, intended to live in communion with God, was now alienated from the ultimate source of all life, joy, peace and fulfillment, but God did not abandon us. Motivated by love, mercy and kindness, he set into action a plan which would meet our need for forgiveness, reconciliation and restoration, and through which justice would be served, wrath satisfied and lavish salvation made available to us. Fast forward...

Abraham

Out of all the people of the world, God chooses one

person to bless in a special way. God adopts Abraham and his descendants as his own people. Abraham's family becomes a tribe and then a nation. God loves them, shepherds them, separates them from the surrounding cultures and begins to teach them about himself. Fast forward...

Passover

Generations come and go, and the descendants of Abraham, after traveling to Egypt to escape a famine and, after enjoying a time of prosperity, are enslaved by the Egyptian people. Eventually, after many years, God acts through his servant Moses to set his people free, but convincing the Egyptians to give up their slaves wasn't easy. After sending a series of plagues upon the Egyptians, God prepares one final plague, and institutes a ritual by which his people will be kept safe and by which they will forever celebrate their freedom from captivity.

Before their last meal in Egypt, God directs the Israelites to slaughter a lamb and to sprinkle its blood on the doorposts of the house. That evening, an Angel of Death will "pass over" every house that has been marked with the blood of a lamb, sparing everyone inside, but visiting death upon the first born in every home that is not marked with the lamb's blood. Fast forward...

Prophets and the law

God sends prophets through whom he represents himself to his people. Through the prophets, God gives a law which reflects his own good and righteous nature. The prophets tell the people of the blessings which will flow from their obedience to God and of the consequences which will follow if they are disobedient. A pattern emerges as the people stray from God, suffer the consequences, cry out for relief and are received back into God's favor. The cycle is repeated again and again.

But there will come a time, the prophets foretell, when God will do something new: He will send a savior, a messiah who will turn the people's hearts back to him for good. Of this coming one, the prophet Isaiah wrote:

For to us a child is born,
  to us a son is given,
  and the government will be on his shoulders.
And he will be called
  Wonderful Counselor, Mighty God,
  Everlasting Father, Prince of Peace.

Meanwhile...

Priests and sacrifices

God ordains priests for his people. The function of the priest is to represent the people to God. Through the priests, God institutes a ritual of animal sacrifice as a means of teaching about sin and forgiveness for sin. To receive forgiveness, a person who was sorry for their sins would take from their flock an animal, free from defect, (a goat or a lamb, for instance) to the priest who would sacrifice it on the altar to God. Through this ritual God taught his people that forgiveness of sin was a costly and bloody affair.

Once a year, on the Day of Atonement, the high priest, after purifying himself, would go behind the curtain in the temple into the Holy of Holies and offer a sacrifice, a perfect lamb, for the sake of all the people.

Years and years pass. The people, sometimes faithful,

sometimes not, wander away from God and are called back by the prophets. God blesses and punishes, the priests make sacrifices, the prophets continue to speak of the one who is coming…. Fast forward...

The First Thing:
Our Need

We are lost, separated from God, sinful, fallen, destined for an eternity apart from God.

The Second Thing:
God's Response to Our Need

The Salvation Gift Package

The Third Thing:
God's Motivation for Responding to Our Need

God responds to our need out of love, mercy and kindness

The Fourth Thing:
The Price God Paid for Our Salvation
(What It Cost God to Purchase Salvation for Us)

Chapter

8

The Fourth Thing:
The Price God Paid for Our Salvation
(Part Three)

The Cross In Its Context

...at just the right time, when we were still powerless,
Christ died for the ungodly.

A child is born, a son is given. The time for fulfillment of the prophesies has come. Jesus is born in Bethlehem and then raised in Nazareth. Years pass...

Baptism

Jesus, now an adult, is ready to begin his ministry. He goes to the Jordan river to be baptized by his cousin John. When John sees him he declares, "Behold, the Lamb of God who takes away the sins of the world."

After Jesus is baptized, as he is coming up out of the water, the heavens are opened, the Spirit descends to Jesus like a dove and a voice says, "This is my son whom I love. With him I am well pleased."

The verb translated "opened" as in "the heavens are opened" is a form of the Greek word "schizo". At Jesus' baptism, the heavens are torn open. Something new is underway.

Ministry and self revelation

Jesus gathers to himself twelve disciples. As they travel together, Jesus heals the sick, feeds the hungry, casts out demons, demonstrates a complete command over nature and teaches about God and all things in relationship to God. Time and time again, as Jesus' great power is demonstrated in a kind and merciful manner, his disciples are left to murmur to themselves, "Who is this man?"

As Jesus teaches, he paints a picture of a loving God who desires the best for us, but who will not tolerate the destructive nature of sin. He urges people to turn their lives around, to forsake their sinful ways, and while his words regarding sin are harsh, his attitude toward sinners is one of deep compassion.

As time goes by, those closest to him begin to piece together who he is: They have seen him do things that can only be done with God's power, they have heard him say things that only God should say and they have heard him make claims about himself that only God can claim. But how could this be...?

And then, just as they're beginning to grasp who they have in their midst, Jesus reveals that which is unthinkable to them. His mission is not to establish a political Kingdom, nor is it to just teach and preach about the love of God and the need to turn from sinfulness. Jesus has come to die for sinners, to give his life as a ransom for many. Only later, after Jesus' resurrection, would his disciples fully understand what had taken place.

The cross within its context

At just the right time, when all had been prepared, the

second person of the Trinity, God the Son, entered into human history. Having God's nature from all eternity and acquiring human nature through his mother Mary, Jesus became one of us. Because he was God, Jesus was the perfect prophet, able to fully reveal God to us, and because he had taken on human nature, Jesus became the perfect priest, able to fully represent humanity to God.

After thirty years of living a life deeply connected to God his Father and after three years of public ministry, Jesus did what no earthly priest could do. Having identified with us by becoming human, Jesus offered a sacrifice for our sins—not the sacrifice of a flawless goat or lamb, but of himself. Jesus the Son of God became the Lamb of God who takes away the sins of the world. The perfect priest offered himself as the perfect sacrifice.

On the night before he was crucified, Jesus celebrated Passover with his disciples, but instead of attending to the ancient ritual, Jesus began a new one. Taking a loaf of bread, he broke it, saying, "this is my body, broken for you". Taking the cup of wine, he said, "this is my blood, shed for you". By so doing, Jesus was declaring himself to be the passover lamb, the shedding of whose blood would protect those within his household.

This was God's solution to the love/wrath dilemma: God himself became human so that he could pay the price for humanity's sinfulness. On the cross, Jesus bore the wrath of God for us. By becoming human, Jesus was identified with us and was thus able to represent us to God. God, out of great love for us, found a way to punish sin and serve justice such that, in Jesus, the punishment fell on himself and not on us.

The Bible records that as Jesus' life drew to a close, he uttered the word "telestai" and then bowed his head and gave up his spirit. "Telestai"—paid in full; Jesus accomplished what he had come to do. Our sin debt was paid in full. At that very moment, the curtain in the temple was torn (schizo) from top to bottom. Just as the heavens were torn open at the beginning of Jesus' ministry, so was the temple curtain torn when he died— the barrier that separated humanity from the presence of God was torn in two.

In the fifty-third chapter of Isaiah, Isaiah prophesies hundreds of years before the birth of Jesus:

...He was pierced for our transgressions,
  he was crushed for our iniquities;
the punishment that brought us peace was on him,
  and by his wounds we are healed.
We all, like sheep, have gone astray,
  each of us has turned to our own way;
and the LORD has laid on him
  the iniquity of us all.

On the cross, Jesus fulfilled this prophecy.

Some two thousand years ago a man was crucified by Roman soldiers on a hillside just outside the city of Jerusalem. While some celebrated and some mourned the death of Jesus of Nazareth, no one realized that the central event of human history had just unfolded. Jesus' death was not the result of unforeseen circumstances, nor was it a tragic ending to a man who inadvertently ended up in the middle of a political and religious conflict. It was part of the plan—God's plan for our salvation— from the beginning.

*　*　*

Jesus died for us on the cross, but neither the cross nor

his death is the end of the story—on the third day, God the Father raised Jesus from the dead. Jesus, the one who died for us, now lives for us and is available to walk through life with us.

Because of Jesus and all he accomplished, every barrier has been removed and every resource necessary for an abundant life fully connected to God has been provided. Salvation has come and is available to us.

The First Thing:
Our Need

We are lost, separated from God, sinful, fallen, destined for an eternity apart from God.

The Second Thing:
God's Response to Our Need

The Salvation Gift Package

The Third Thing:
God's Motivation for Responding to Our Need

God responds to our need out of love, mercy and kindness

The Fourth Thing:
The Price God Paid for Our Salvation
(What It Cost God to Purchase Salvation for Us)

On the cross, Jesus represents us and fully bears the wrath of God for us. Jesus' sacrificial death on the cross pays the penalty for our sinfulness. His death purchases for us and makes available to us all the gifts within the Salvation Gift Package.

The Fifth Thing:
The Price at Which Salvation Is Offered to Us
(What It Costs Us to Receive Salvation.)

Chapter

9

The Fifth Thing:
**The Price at Which God Offers
Salvation to Us**

Grace

...it is by grace you have been saved.

We've all seen the movies where someone, dying of thirst in the desert, drops to their knees and crawls until they collapse, where they stay until they die—unless someone comes along to save them. Imagine you're that person, but instead of collapsing, you manage to crawl your way to my refreshment stand where I have available large amounts of cool, refreshing water—for a price.

What price? Well, if my water supply cost me a considerable amount to acquire, it would be fair to pass that amount along to you. And it would certainly be reasonable to add something for my trouble. But since I have something you desperately need, I'm in a position to demand whatever I think you'll be willing to pay, and you'll be willing to pay whatever I ask.

The important thing to note is that what it cost me to acquire the water you need and the price at which I offer it to you are two different things. Even if the cost to me is minimal, I may still take advantage of your desperate situation and charge you a huge amount. Or, though the cost to me is great, I may have mercy on you and offer the water to you for free.

We've seen the great lengths God had to go to purchase our salvation—the cost to him was extreme. But what will it cost us to acquire salvation from God? At what price does God offer salvation to us?

We are warned that if something seems too good to be true it probably is. Perhaps that is why we have such a hard time grasping that God, having paid dearly for our salvation, offers it to us for free. God's gift of salvation is too good to be true and it's true. This tremendous act of generosity is what the Bible calls grace. We are saved not because of something we did or promise to do; we are saved because God, out of his kindness and mercy, purchased salvation for us and graciously offers it to us as a gift. Salvation is a free gift. We are saved by God's generosity. We are saved by his grace.

* * *

We're not likely to appreciate the richness of the salvation gift package God offers to us if we don't understand the depth of our need. And we won't be able to appreciate the extent of God's grace if we aren't aware of the price he paid to bring salvation to us. Understanding each of salvation's six things will enhance our appreciation and understanding of the other five. Attempting to understand the six things of salvation in isolation will almost certainly result in misunderstanding.

It's also important to distinguish between the six things if we are to avoid confusion. As we have seen, what it cost God to purchase the salvation gift package for us is distinct from what it costs us to acquire it from him. And the cost to us to acquire salvation from God is distinct from how we acquire it.

This last thought bears further reflection because many

assume that because salvation is offered to us as a free gift, we automatically enjoy its benefits, but this is not the case.

If you're concerned about getting a sunburn and a friend offers you some of their sunscreen, the sunscreen, although it's offered to you for free, won't protect you unless you apply it. Likewise (going back to our dying-of-thirst-in-the-desert story), the water that is given to you freely will not save you unless you drink it.

It is the same with the salvation gift package: It must be received if we are to enjoy its many benefits. How we receive salvation is the subject of the next three chapters.

The First Thing:
Our Need

We are lost, separated from God, sinful, fallen, destined for an eternity apart from God.

The Second Thing:
God's Response to Our Need

The Salvation Gift Package

The Third Thing:
God's Motivation for Responding to Our Need

God responds to our need out of love, mercy and kindness

The Fourth Thing:
The Price God Paid for Our Salvation
(What It Cost God to Purchase Salvation for Us)

On the cross, Jesus represents us and fully bears the wrath of God for us. Jesus' sacrificial death on the cross pays the penalty for our sinfulness. His death purchases for us and makes available to us all the gifts within the Salvation Gift Package.

The Fifth Thing:
The Price at Which Salvation Is Offered to Us
(What It Costs Us to Receive Salvation.)

Salvation is offered to us as a free gift, by grace.

The Six Thing:
How Salvation Is Received

Chapter

10

The Sixth Thing:
How Salvation Is Received
(Part One)

Faith, Ordinary Faith

Therefore, since we have been justified
through faith, we have peace with God...

What an odd thing it would be to sit across the table from someone as they ate a bucket of chicken all the while insisting that, while eating may be all right for you, it's not something they practice or need. Wouldn't it be strange to hear someone deny engaging in a behavior which they unwittingly engage in several times a day? Yet so it is with faith.

Scripture teaches that we are saved *through faith* which makes it crucial that we understand both what faith is and how we're saved through it. But while faith and its role in salvation are easily understood, confusion about faith is common and runs deep.

What is faith? Faith is trust. To put your faith in someone or something is to trust them. When you trust someone (or something), you're putting faith in them (or it). Consider the following four scenarios:

Scenario one: Sending a package

If you want to send a package to a friend in New York,

you'll need to trust the delivery service with the package. When you slide the package across the counter, you're putting faith in the delivery service to treat your package with care and to deliver it as promised. Your faith may be reasonable or unreasonable: If the delivery service has a reputation and a track record for good service, your faith is reasonable, but if the delivery service is run by a shady looking character working out of the back of a rusty van, your faith is, in all likelihood, unreasonable.

Scenario two: Traveling by air

If you decide to fly to New York to visit a friend, you'll need to put your faith in an airline. Getting on an airplane is a major act of faith: You're trusting it (along with the flight and maintenance crews) with your life. Is trusting an airline with your life reasonable? It depends on the airline: If the airline has a good safety record your faith is reasonable. But if the airline is under investigation for falsifying safety records and skimping on maintenance, your faith would be unreasonable.

Scenario three: Dentistry

If you have a tooth that is causing you pain, you'll need to consent to the treatment and you'll need to sit back in the dental chair and open your mouth. Opening your mouth to the dentist is an act of faith: You're trusting that they'll fix what's wrong (and not make things worse) while keeping your discomfort to a minimum. Is your faith reasonable? If the dentist comes highly recommended and behaves in a professional manner, if the diplomas on the wall are in order and the instruments appear clean, your faith is probably justified. But if there are flies buzzing around the office, the diplomas appear to be filled out in pencil and the instruments are filthy and rusty, your faith would be contrary to the evidence.

Scenario four: Surgery

Submitting to heart surgery is an act of faith: In lying back on the operating table you're consenting to allow someone to make you unconscious and another to cut you open with a knife. That's faith! Is it reasonable faith? Again it depends: If the surgeon is accredited and experienced, then yes, it is reasonable. But if the surgeon is operating out of someone's garage, well....

In each of the above scenarios, someone trusts something of value (a package, their life) to someone or something (a surgeon, an airline) in the hope of getting a desired result (the package delivered, relief from pain, a return to health). In each case, the desired result cannot occur without an act of faith. The package will not be delivered unless you hand it over to the delivery service. You cannot travel by air to New York unless you step on an airplane. Your tooth cannot be fixed unless you open your mouth to the dentist. Your heart cannot be surgically repaired unless you lie back on the operating table.

In light of the above, two things should be clear: First, faith is not something that only religious people practice, nor is it something necessarily religious in nature. Faith is something everyone practices out of necessity many times daily. Every time you eat at a restaurant, deposit money into a bank account or get in a taxi, you're exercising faith.

Second, faith is not contrary to reason or fact, faith is qualified by reason or fact. Faith can be reasonable or unreasonable. Faith can be exercised in light of the evidence or without regard to the evidence. Faith can take account of the relevant facts or it can ignore them. Faith can be justified or unjustified.

So when someone says, "You go ahead and live by faith, I prefer to live by reason," or, "You religious people and your faith. I prefer fact," they're demonstrating a clear lack of awareness regarding the nature of faith and the degree to which they are *constantly* exercising faith. They are like a person who, while eating a bucket of chicken, insists that they have no use for eating.

Consider a fifth scenario: A father promises to take his daughter to Disneyland in two months as a birthday present. What does the daughter do? She anticipates and begins to prepare for the trip. This, too, is an act of faith. Any time a promise is enjoyed or preparations are made in anticipation of a promise being kept, faith is being exercised.

To summarize this chapter:

• Faith is not just something religious people practice; faith is something everyone practices.

• Faith is not rare or uncommon; faith is a constant of everyday life.

• Mailing a package, traveling by air, submitting to surgery, eating at a restaurant and making preparations in light of a promise all have a faith component, without the exercise of which the desired result could not occur.

• Faith is not contrary to reason or fact; faith is qualified by reason or fact. A particular act of faith may be rational or irrational, but faith itself is neither rational nor irrational.

*　*　*

Some may object that faith in God is different from that which is exhibited in the above examples. They'll note that some religious people seem to define faith such that faith and reason are pitted against each other, as if faith is somehow more praiseworthy when it is based on nothing or when it runs contrary to reason. To this objection I can only respond that, yes, some religious people are just as confused about faith as many nonreligious people. Biblical faith, by contrast, is always encouraged in light of God having demonstrated himself to be trustworthy. We are encouraged to trust God in light of what he has done for us and who he has revealed himself to be. The idea that blind, contrary-to-the-evidence faith is praiseworthy is nowhere to be found in the Bible.

The First Thing:
Our Need

We are lost, separated from God, sinful, fallen, destined for an eternity apart from God.

The Second Thing:
God's Response to Our Need

The Salvation Gift Package

The Third Thing:
God's Motivation for Responding to Our Need

God responds to our need out of love, mercy and kindness

The Fourth Thing:
The Price God Paid for Our Salvation
(What It Cost God to Purchase Salvation for Us)

On the cross, Jesus represents us and fully bears the wrath of God for us. Jesus' sacrificial death on the cross pays the penalty for our sinfulness. His death purchases for us and makes available to us all the gifts within the Salvation Gift Package.

The Fifth Thing:
The Price At Which Salvation Is Offered to Us
(What It Costs Us to Receive Salvation.)

Salvation is offered to us as a free gift, by grace.

The Six Thing:
How Salvation Is Received

Chapter

11

The Sixth Thing:
How Salvation Is Received
(Part Two)

Believing, Believing and Believing

...whoever believes in him
shall not perish but have eternal life.

Do you believe in UFOs? You know, the kind from other planets or solar systems, the kind piloted by space aliens? Do you believe in Santa Claus or the Tooth Fairy or Big Foot or ESP?

Do you believe that $E = mc^2$? Or that Mars has two moons?

Have you ever said to someone, "I believe in you" or, "you've got to believe in yourself"?

Notice how the word "believe" is used differently in the above paragraphs. In the first, "believe" is used in the sense of "to affirm the existence of". To believe in UFOs is to believe in the existence of UFOs. The same is true with Santa Claus and the Tooth Fairy. To believe in them is to believe that they exist.

In the second paragraph, "believe" means "to consider to be true". When someone says that they believe Mars has two moons, they're saying that they consider the statement "Mars has two moons," to be true.

In the third paragraph, "believe" is used in the sense of "to trust in, to have faith in". When a father says to his son, "I know you can do it. I believe in you." he's not making a statement about his son's existence, rather, he's asserting faith in his son's abilities.

Thus, "believe" can mean " to affirm the existence of" or "to consider to be true" or "to trust in, to have faith in".

Understanding the above distinctions matter in light of Jesus' claims that "...whoever *believes* in him [Jesus] shall not perish but have eternal life." But what kind of "believe" does Jesus mean?

Consider the following scenario: You're traveling in Africa when you suffer a heart attack which damages your heart to the extent that you will need open heart surgery if you are to survive. In the next village there is a traveling medical team, a member of which happens to be a surgeon capable of performing the necessary procedure. If your life is to be saved, you must believe in the existence of the surgeon and you must believe that you need the surgery. In other words, you must believe both in the sense of "affirming the existence of" and in the sense of "considering certain things to be true".

But, while believing in both of these ways is necessary for your life to be saved, neither is sufficient to save you unless you also believe in the third sense. To be saved, you must "trust in or have faith in" the surgeon. You must have faith in the surgeon to the extent that you allow him to operate on your heart.

It is the same with the salvation Jesus offers. To be saved we must believe that one exists who is capable and inclined to save us and we must believe that we need to be saved. But believing these things apart from trusting in Jesus will not save us. As with a surgeon, we must believe in Jesus to the extent that we allow him to do his work. We must allow him into our hearts, into the core of our being; we must trust him with our lives. This kind of faith we rightly call saving faith.

*   *   *

While it is beyond the scope of this book to present and consider the evidence for God's existence, I believe such evidence exists and that it is compelling. For those for whom the existence of God is an open question, I've included a list of resources in the appendix for your consideration.

The First Thing:
Our Need

We are lost, separated from God, sinful, fallen, destined for an eternity apart from God.

The Second Thing:
God's Response to Our Need

The Salvation Gift Package

The Third Thing:
God's Motivation for Responding to Our Need

God responds to our need out of love, mercy and kindness

The Fourth Thing:
The Price God Paid for Our Salvation
(What It Cost God to Purchase Salvation for Us)

On the cross, Jesus represents us and fully bears the wrath of God for us. Jesus' sacrificial death on the cross pays the penalty for our sinfulness. His death purchases for us and makes available to us all the gifts within the Salvation Gift Package.

The Fifth Thing:
The Price at Which Salvation Is Offered to Us

Salvation is offered to us as a free gift, by grace.

The Six Thing:
How Salvation Is Received

Chapter

12

The Sixth Thing:
How Salvation Is Received
(Part Three)

Saving Faith

For it is by grace you have been saved, through faith...

In the preceding chapters we've used examples from everyday (and not-so-everyday) life to help us understand and clarify what faith is. Through them we've seen that faith cannot be confined to a religious context, that it is a common and necessary part of our everyday existence, that very little could be accomplished without it and that it can (and should) be informed by evidence and reason. As we turn our attention to saving faith, these examples still have a few things to teach us.

Faith is exercised with a desired result in mind, but it must be properly placed and appropriately expressed for the desired result to be realized. If the desired result is a surgically repaired heart, faith is properly placed in a surgeon and appropriately expressed by lying back on the operating table. If the desired result is getting to New York by air, faith is properly placed in an airline and appropriately expressed by getting on the plane.

Without faith, the desired result cannot be realized, but faith itself doesn't do the work, it doesn't accomplish anything on its own, it merely allows the work to take place. The power of faith, therefore, does not reside in faith itself, but in the person or thing in which faith is placed. Faith, even great faith, which is misplaced or inappropriately expressed, will not result in that which is desired. If surgery is required, you need to place faith in a surgeon not the postal service, and you need to express faith by lying back on the operating table, not by handing a package over to a postal worker.

When Jesus said to those who had come to him for healing, *"your faith has saved you"*, he was not praising faith in general, but faith in *him*. When Jesus, referring to himself, said, "...whoever *believes in him* shall not perish, but have eternal life," it was in the context of encouraging his listeners to place their faith in him for salvation.

Saving faith is faith which is properly placed in the one who alone has the power to save. Only Jesus died on our behalf and only Jesus can give us the benefits of the salvation gift package he purchased for us. Saving faith is faith which is properly placed in Jesus.

How is saving faith appropriately expressed? To explore this question, we'll return to our everyday examples once again. As previously noted, with surgery, faith is appropriately expressed by lying back on the operating table. With dentistry, faith is appropriately expressed by opening one's mouth to the dentist. With air travel, faith is appropriately expressed by getting on the airplane. But if we look more closely, we'll see that these expressions of faith are but the most overt in what is often a series of faith expressions—all of which may be necessary for the desired result to be realized.

Depending on the desired result, faith may find its expression in one or all of the following actions:

Seeking or approaching

Asking or inviting
Giving consent or permission
Granting access or surrendering

If the desired result is a surgically repaired heart, for example, you must go to the surgeon (seeking or approaching), sign the consent forms (giving consent or permission) and lie back on the operating table (granting access or surrendering). Each is an expression of faith without which the desired result cannot be realized.

Likewise, if you desire salvation, saving faith is expressed by seeking or approaching Jesus, asking or inviting him to save you, giving him consent or permission to save you and granting him access to or surrendering your life to him to be saved.

More specifically, and, in light of the many components of the salvation gift package, when we learn of our need and of Jesus' offer, we approach Jesus for salvation. He offers to forgive, justify and redeem us and we ask him to do so. He offers to adopt us into his family and we consent. He offers to bring about our spiritual rebirth and we give him permission. He expresses his desire to commune with us and live in us through his Holy Spirit and we invite him into our hearts. He offers to complete and bring to fruition in our lives his saving work and we surrender ourselves to him. Such is saving faith's proper expression.

But the above must be qualified in light of Jesus' generosity and grace. While there are times when faith's expression must be full and complete for a desired result to be realized (surgery, for instance, will not take place unless the consent forms are properly filled out and signed), salvation does not depend upon the perfection or strength of our faith because the one who died to purchase salvation for us eagerly desires that we should come to possess it.

Without some knowledge of our need and of the salvation God offers to us, no one would turn to Jesus to be saved, but few, if any, understand the fullness of the salvation gift package or exactly what they're about when they first confess their sin, ask for forgiveness or invite Jesus into their hearts. Yet, Jesus gives the fullness of his salvation to those who ask before they understand the fullness of what they're asking for.

When we appropriately express our faith in him, Jesus does for us what we cannot do for ourselves and one of the things we can't do is appropriately express our faith in him. In our brokenness, we cannot wholeheartedly consent to receive all that he has for us, invite him into our hearts or surrender to his care. Yet Jesus, despite our ignorance and inability, graciously accepts what we bring to him. Jesus responds to the incompleteness of our faith with complete and full salvation.

13

An Overview of Salvation's Six Things

The First Thing:

Our Need

We are:

Lost
Separated from God
Sinful
Fallen
Destined for an eternity apart from God.

The Second Thing:

God's Response to Our Need

God responds to our need with the Salvation Gift Package. The Salvation Gift Package includes:

Forgiveness
Justification
Redemption
Adoption
Spiritual rebirth
Eternal life
The Holy Spirit is given:

To live in and through us
To stay with us
To comfort us
To lead us into truth

To be our advocate
To equip us for service
To make us like Jesus
To testify to us that we really are God's
children.

The Third Thing:

God's Motivation for Responding to Our Need

God responds to our need out of:

Love
Mercy
And kindness

The Fourth Thing:

The Price God Paid for Our Salvation
(What It Cost God to Purchase Salvation for Us)

On the cross, Jesus represents us and fully bears the wrath of God for us. Jesus' sacrificial death on the cross pays the penalty for our sinfulness. His death purchases for us and makes available to us all the gifts within the Salvation Gift Package.

The Fifth Thing:

The Price at Which Salvation Is Offered to Us

Salvation is offered to us as a free gift, by grace.

The Six Thing:

How Salvation Is Received

Salvation is received by placing faith in Jesus for salvation. (By trusting in Jesus to save us.)

* * *

This book is organized around the framework of "just six things (then a seventh)" as opposed to "just seven things" because blurring the lines between the seventh thing and the other six can lead to an error which seriously undermines the entire project. What I mean by this and why this is so will become apparent after we've explored the seventh thing.

In the next chapter, we'll examine some of the biblical texts upon which the six things are founded. Some readers may be tempted to skip this chapter or give it only a cursory reading, but I would ask you not to do so. It is important to understand that the six things as I've presented them are not a product of my imagination or a projection of my preferences and desires, but are rather an accurate reflection of what the Bible teaches.

After examining the salvation texts, we'll explore the seventh thing in chapters fifteen and sixteen.

Chapter

14

The Salvation Texts

Up to this point, I've presented the six things with minimal reference to scripture and this deserves an explanation. Within the salvation texts (those texts which reference one or more of the six things), the six things are often intertwined with each other; they're described in rich and varied language, and they're presented not necessarily in any particular order. This can make it difficult, especially for those who are unfamiliar with the Bible or with Christian theology, to piece together a clear picture of salvation directly from the texts.

In my work with those who are unfamiliar with the Bible, I've found that when I provide the biblical framework of the six things before going to scripture, the pieces of the salvation puzzle fall together much more quickly and with deeper comprehension and retention than when I begin with scripture alone.

* * *

As previously noted, salvation texts are biblical texts which reference one or more of the six things: 1) our need, 2) God's response to our need, 3) God's motivation for responding to our need, 4) the price God paid for our salvation (what it cost God to purchase salvation for us), 5) the price at which salvation is offered to us (what it costs us to receive salvation) and 6) how salvation is received.

Having established the six biblical categories, we'll now

turn to examine some of the salvation texts upon which they're grounded.

As an aid to recognizing the six things, I've labeled them within brackets. For example, John 3: 16 begins, "For God so loved the world..." which speaks of God's motivation for responding to our need as he does. Since this is the third thing, it appears as follows: "For [God so loved the world3]". Likewise, Romans 5: 1 appears as follows:

"Therefore, since [we have been justified2] [through faith6], we have peace with God through our Lord Jesus Christ..."

because justification is part of the salvation gift package (the second thing) and faith is how we receive salvation (the sixth thing).

Take time to get to know the following verses. (If you find the brackets distracting, you can look the verses up in a Bible.)

* * *

John 3: 16
For [God so loved the world3] that he [[gave5] his one and only Son4], that [whoever believes in him6] shall not [perish1] but have [eternal life2].

Romans 3: 23 - 25
...for [all have sinned and fall short of the glory of God1], and all [are justified2] [freely by his grace5] through the [redemption2] that came by Christ Jesus. [God presented Christ as a sacrifice of atonement, through the shedding of his blood4] —[to be received by faith6].

80

Romans 6: 23

[For the wages of sin is death1], but the [gift of God5] is [eternal life2] in Christ Jesus our Lord.

Ephesians 2: 1 - 10

As for you, [you were dead in your transgressions and sins1], in which you used to live when you followed the ways of this world... All of us also lived among them at one time, gratifying the cravings of our flesh and following its desires and thoughts. Like the rest, [we were by nature deserving of wrath1]. But [because of his great love for us, God, who is rich in mercy3], [made us alive with Christ2] even when [we were dead in transgressions1]—[it is by grace5] [you have been saved2]. And [God raised us up with Christ and seated us with him in the heavenly realms2] in Christ Jesus, in order that in the coming ages he might show [the incomparable riches of his grace5], [expressed in his kindness to us in Christ Jesus3]. For [it is by grace5] [you have been saved2], [through faith6]—and this is not from yourselves, [it is the gift of God—not by works5], so that no one can boast. For we are God's handiwork, created in Christ Jesus to do good works, which God prepared in advance for us to do.

Galatians 4: 3b - 7

[...we were in slavery under the elemental spiritual forces of the world1]. But when the set time had fully come, [God sent his Son4], born of a woman, born under the law, [to redeem2] those under the law, [that we might receive adoption to sonship2]. Because you are his sons, [God sent the Spirit of his Son into our hearts2], the Spirit who calls out, "Abba, Father." [So you are no longer a slave, but God's child; and since you are his child, God has made you also an heir2].

Colossians 1: 13, 14

For [he has rescued us[2]] [from the dominion of darkness[1]] and [brought us into the kingdom of the Son he loves[2]], [in whom we have redemption[2]], [the forgiveness of sins[2]].

Romans 5: 1

Therefore, since [we have been justified[2]] [through faith[6]], we have peace with God through our Lord Jesus Christ,

Titus 3:5

...[he saved us[2]], not because of righteous things we had done, but [because of his mercy[3]]. [He saved us through the washing of rebirth and renewal by the Holy Spirit[2]],

Romans 8: 15 - 16

[The Spirit you received[2]] does not make you slaves, so that you live in fear again; rather, [the Spirit you received brought about your adoption to sonship[2]]. And by him we cry, "Abba, Father." [The Spirit himself testifies with our spirit that we are God's children[2]].

Colossians 2:13, 14

13 [When you were dead in your sins and in the uncircumcision of your flesh[1]], [God made you alive with Christ[2]]. [He forgave us all our sins, 14 having canceled the charge of our legal indebtedness[1]], which stood against us and condemned us; [he has taken it away, nailing it to the cross[4]].

1 John 3: 1

See [what great love the Father has lavished on us[3]], [that we should be called children of God! And that is what we are[2]]!

1 John 4: 9 - 10

This is how [God showed his love among us[3]]: [He sent his one and only Son into the world[4]] that we might live through him. This is love: not that we loved God, but that [he loved us[3]] [and sent his Son as an atoning sacrifice for our sins[4]].

* * *

If we group the various parts of the salvation texts together, here's what emerges:

The first thing: **Our need** (in whole or in part): We were sinful, dead in transgressions, under judgement, deserving of wrath, in slavery to the spiritual forces of the world within the dominion of darkness. Living in fear, we were perishing and condemned.

The second thing: **God's response to our need** (the salvation gift package in whole or in part): We are saved, forgiven, justified, redeemed, rescued, brought into Christ's kingdom, made alive and raised up with Christ. Our sin has been atoned for. We are at peace with God. We have been sent and have received into our hearts the Holy Spirit who washes and renews us and who brings about our spiritual rebirth. We are adopted into God's family (and are called and truly are) children of God. We are heirs of God for all eternity.

The third thing: **God's motivation for responding to our need as he does**: God saves us out of his great love, kindness and mercy.

The fourth thing: **The price God paid for our salvation** (what it cost God to purchase salvation for us): God sent his one and only Son into the world as an atoning sacrifice for our sins.

Christ's blood was shed, taking away our legal indebtedness, canceling it. God sends the Spirit of his Son (the Holy Spirit) into our hearts.

The fifth thing: **The price at which salvation is offered to us**: Freely, by grace.

The sixth thing: **How we receive the salvation God offers to us**: By faith, through faith, by believing in him (Jesus).

In summary, God, because of his great love, kindness and mercy, when we were dead in transgressions and deserving of wrath, saved us by sending his Son Jesus to atone for our sin —the results of which he offers to us freely, by grace to be received by faith in Jesus.

* * *

Note that the texts referenced above were written to those who had already received salvation. This is why they speak of our need and of our having received salvation in the past tense. Do not be confused on this point: All who put their faith in Jesus have received salvation; those who haven't done so (or who have yet to do so) are not saved.

If you are a woman, don't be put off by the "adoption to sonship" language. Such language sounds exclusionary to modern ears, but it merely reflects the custom at the time it was written. It is entirely appropriate to render the above as "adoption to sonship and daughtership". (And just as a side note: Scripture sometimes uses metaphors which require men to make a mental adjustment to include themselves as when believers are collectively referred to as "the bride of Christ".)

Finally, let me state unequivocally that the truthfulness

and authority of the previous chapters in this book rests upon these verses, for in the other chapters I have attempted to make clear the truth as set forth in these texts and nothing more. What I have written stands or falls in light of these verses and what I have written should be judged by them and not the other way around.

Chapter

15

The Seventh Thing:
Embracing Salvation
(Part One)

On Gifts and Giving

In the first chapter, we considered how a homeless man's life could be changed by the inheritance gifts he received: The gifts of a home, security, medical care, abundant food, spending money, and the like. But we noted that coming into possession of the gifts would not automatically bring about the intended change of lifestyle. It's entirely possible for a homeless person, despite newfound wealth, to continue to live a life of homelessness. A bed with clean sheets in a warm home does not preclude one from sleeping on the cold streets. Gifts can be received and then ignored; gifts can be received and then forgotten. For an inheritance to change the life of a homeless person as intended, the inheritance gifts must be *embraced*.

At the heart of salvation's six things lies the salvation gift package. The gifts are intended by God to bring us into the fullness of life God intends for us to have and enjoy. But, merely receiving the gifts will not accomplish the fullness of life God intends for us. For that to happen, the salvation gifts must be embraced.

This, then, is the essence of the seventh thing: Embracing the gifts of the salvation gift package such that they bring us into the fullness of life God intends.

But how do we embrace the gifts of the salvation gift package? The answer is not as simple as we might expect, because the nature of gifts and giving is complex, and the salvation gifts are many and diverse in nature. In this chapter, we'll consider the nature of gifts and giving in general. In the next, we'll apply what we've learned specifically to the salvation gifts.

* * *

Gifts are free and any "gift" that requires payment, either before or after the receipt of the gift, is not really a gift at all. Gifts are free of any obligation regarding payment or repayment.

But while gifts are free of payment obligation, they are not free of the intention of the giver. A few years ago, a scruffy looking man sitting outside a convenience store asked me for money. Having been advised not to give money in such circumstances, I asked the man if he was hungry. He said "yes" and so I bought him a sandwich, a bag of chips and a bottle of orange juice. Returning to my car, I made a phone call before driving off and while on the phone, I watched as the man got up and went back into the store. After what appeared to be a discussion with the clerk, he exited the store, not with the sandwich, but with a pack of cigarettes.

The gift I gave the man was intended to satisfy his hunger, not his craving for nicotine. Because the sandwich was a gift, the man had no obligation to pay me for it, but, having received it, he did have an obligation to embrace the intention for which I gave it. It is the same with all gifts: Upon receiving them, we are expected to embrace the intention for which they were given. When a parent gives their son or daughter money for tuition, their intention is that the money be used for tuition and not on a road trip to Vegas. The son or daughter does not have an obligation to repay the gift, but they are obligated to embrace their parent's intentions by using the money as intended.

Embracing the intention for which a gift is given can be as easy as eating a sandwich. (That is, in fact, how the gift of a sandwich is embraced.) But some gifts require an extensive investment of time, energy and commitment in order to embrace the purpose for which they are given. When a grandparent pays for their grandchild's medical school, for instance, the purpose of the gift will not be fulfilled without a disciplined and extensive investment of time and energy on the part of the recipient. The effort is not to pay for the gift, it's to embrace the intended purpose of the gift.

How a gift is embraced is directly related to the nature of the gift and the intention with which it is given. Consider each of the following:

A popsicle
A smoke detector
A gym membership
A club membership
A first aid kit

Of the above, one is embraced by eating it (the popsicle), another by sweating (the gym membership). One is embraced by attaching it to the ceiling (the smoke detector) and another by enjoying the rights and privileges it confers (the club membership). And one of the above is intended to never be used at all (the first aid kit)—it's embraced by keeping it nearby just in case.

If a gift is intended to be enjoyed, we embrace the gift by enjoying it. If it is intended to be eaten, we embrace it by eating it. If a gift confers rights and responsibilities, we embrace it by asserting those rights and by accepting the responsibilities. If a gift confers new life, we embrace the new life by nurturing it. And so forth….

To summarize:

• Gifts, true gifts, are always free of any payment or repayment obligation.

• Gifts are given for an intended purpose which the recipient is obligated to embrace.

• Some gifts require effort for their intended purpose to be fulfilled.

• How a gift is embraced is directly related to the nature of the gift and the intention for which the gift is given.

* * *

I want to close with a story, the purpose of which will become apparent in the next chapter.

A man walks into the apple orchard he has just purchased. When he reaches the center, he says, "Listen up all you apples trees. As the new owner, I want to make sure we're all on the same page. I want you to know that I understand what my job is and you need to know what I expect from you."

There was silence in the orchard as the man paused briefly. "I'll be making sure you get all the water you need. I'll be pruning you once a year and I'll make sure you're protected from frost in the winter. You are all very valuable to me and I want you to know that I'll be treating you accordingly."

The man continued: "Here's what I expect from you: I want you to sink your roots deep—really get down into the water table. I want you to spread your branches tall and wide so that all your leaves are exposed to the sunshine. And then I want you to produce apples—big, red, juicy apples." This all sounded good to the trees and they excitedly murmured in approval.

Then the man called the dogs to him and said, "Okay dogs, I've got a special task for you. You know the dirt road that runs past the orchard? I want every car that travels past to have a security escort. Make a lot of noise in the process—really let them know that you're on the job. Oh, and I'd love it if you'd play a game of fetch with me every now and then."

As you might imagine, the dogs were very pleased with their assignment. Calling the cats, the man said, "I've got just one job for you: Keep the rodent population under control. So long as do this, you can sleep in the sunshine as much as you want."

The dogs, cats and trees were all very pleased because the owner of the orchard gave each of them tasks for which they were suited by their nature.

Chapter

16

The Seventh Thing:
Embracing Salvation
(Part Two)

Embracing the Salvation Gifts

The gifts of the salvation gift package are intended by God to bring us into the fullness of life he intends for us to have and enjoy—a life of abiding love, joy, peace and goodness, a life that can only be found in God, because God himself is the source of these things. Just as life for a fish can only be found in water, the fullness of life God intends for us can only be found in a relationship with him. This is why the salvation gifts are relational in nature; they are intended to restore, renew and make possible the kind of relationship with God that God desires us to have and enjoy.

Merely receiving the gifts is not enough to bring us into the fullness of this relationship—the gifts must be embraced. In the previous chapter, we noted that how a gift is embraced is related to the nature of the gift and the intention with which the gift is given. Because each gift in the salvation gift package is unique and intended to accomplish something unique, each gift is to be uniquely embraced.

The purpose of this chapter is not to provide a practical, step-by-step guide for embracing the gifts, but to note the different ways the gifts are embraced and the effort required to do so.

Forgiveness

In my seventh grade year, I played a major role in the extended humiliation of someone who had been a friend. It is, as far as I am aware, the most shameful thing I've ever done and I deeply regret my behavior even to this day. Decades later, I had a conversation with a woman who was distressed because her daughter was being picked on at school by her peers. As I listened, it occurred to me that my sin against my friend had not been against him only, but against his family and all those who cared about him, including God.

It is not possible to sin against someone in isolation. The man who commits adultery sins against his wife, his children, his wife's family and God—all are impacted. God is always a party to our sin. As great as my sin toward my friend was, it's nothing compared to the totality of my sin against the God from whom nothing is hidden.

A subject who commits and is known to commit treason against his king is not likely to enjoy being in the presence of his king, any more than a known adulterer would enjoy being in the presence of his wife's family. God desires for us to enter into, enjoy, and live in his presence, but it's not possible to enjoy God's presence while in the presence of our sin. By forgiving us, God sets us free—free from sin and free to enjoy life with him.

We receive forgiveness by acknowledging and confessing our sin, trusting that God will forgive us as he has promised. We embrace forgiveness by entering into God's presence, confident that the record of our sin has been erased, knowing that when we look into his eyes, we will never see condemnation, rejection or wrath.

Justification

It's said that the Las Vegas casinos use face recognition software to identify those who come onto their property. Apparently they can link repeat customers to a file containing information about their previous visits. The file might reveal a person's past criminal activity or identify them as a big spender. As you can imagine, a big spender would get a very different reception from casino personnel than someone who has a history of cheating. If we were to gain access to a notorious cheater's file, erase the record of their cheating and replace it with the record of the casino's best customer, what a surprise welcome they'd receive!

Forgiveness and justification, together, are like that. With forgiveness, the record of our sin is erased. With justification, we are identified with Jesus such that his faithfulness and goodness are credited to our account. Forgiveness means that we can go into God's presence free of our sin and without fear of his condemnation, rejection or wrath. Justification means that we can go into God's presence anticipating nothing but his welcome, approval and delight.

Little is required for us to embrace forgiveness and justification. They are gateway gifts which make possible and welcome us into communion with God, and we embrace them by simply entering into God's presence and enjoying communion with him.

Adoption

With adoption, God reveals that he is not satisfied to welcome us into his presence as forgiven and justified servants. He wants to bring us into his family as chosen, beloved sons and daughters. And because God is rightly called king, we become, through adoption, children of the king, sons and daughters of royalty, heirs to the kingdom of heaven.

With adoption into God's family comes privileges and responsibilities. Our privileges include continuous access to our heavenly father and to the resources which he provides us. Our responsibilities include representing our king and his kingdom well; we are called to be God's ambassadors.

Adoption is the first gift to require something of us to fulfill. Representing God's family, being God's ambassador, will require study, discipline, maturation and commitment.

We embrace adoption by enjoying our status as God's children and by committing ourselves to the process of becoming his faithful ambassadors.

Spiritual Rebirth

Up to this point, the salvation gift package has changed our status and standing before God. It's given us rights, privileges and responsibilities, but it has not yet addressed our deepest need.

I ended chapter fifteen with a story about the owner of an orchard who asked his apple trees to produce apples, his dogs to provide security and his cats to keep the rodent population under control. Because each creature was assigned a task in keeping with its nature, all were pleased with their assignments and enthusiastically set about them.

But, we can imagine what would happen if the creatures were assigned tasks for which their natures were less well suited. Surely the dogs wouldn't be as good at keeping the rodent population under control as the cats, nor would the cats be as good at security as the dogs. And it's possible to assign tasks for which the creatures are completely unsuited. If we asked the cats to produce apples, for instance, or the trees to play fetch, we'd be asking them to do that which their natures simply could not do.

Our deepest need before God is rooted in our fallen nature which simply cannot and does not want to please God. If we are to be and become all God desires us to be and become, we need a new nature—the nature we are born with just isn't up to the task. This is why Jesus said we must be born again and this is why the heart of the salvation gift package, God's response to our need, is spiritual rebirth.

According to the Bible, the new spiritual nature God gives to those who receive the salvation gift package is created to be like Jesus in goodness and faithfulness. What the fallen nature, crippled by sin, is incapable of being and doing, the new nature is and can do.

But the new spiritual nature is not given to us all grown up. As with all things newly born, the new nature requires nurture and time for it to mature. Once mature and fully nurtured, the new nature will produce the spiritual fruits of love, joy, peace, goodness and faithfulness that God desires for us to enjoy and share with others.

How do we embrace spiritual rebirth? By committing ourselves to the process of becoming fully mature men and women of God. This means discovering and embracing our spiritual needs (that which our new spiritual nature needs to grow and mature) and being intentional about meeting those needs.

Maturing into the person God desires us to be is not

always easy, but God does not leave us to struggle on our own. God gives us, through his Holy Spirit, both the new nature and all the necessary resources for its growth and maturation.

The Gift of the Holy Spirit

The Holy Spirit is given to all those who receive salvation, that he might live in and through us, comfort us, help us to mature, guide us into truth, pray with and for us, give us gifts to use for his kingdom's sake, empower us and testify to us that we are God's children.

As I mentioned near the beginning of this chapter, it is beyond the scope of this book to provide more than an overview of how the salvation gifts are embraced, and nowhere is this more true than with the gift of the Holy Spirit. The Spirit's role in the life of those who have received salvation is so vast, diverse and all encompassing that it is difficult to know where to start.

For our purposes, may it suffice to say that we embrace the gift of the Holy Spirit when we...

allow him to live in and through us.

rest in his comfort.

accept his help.

follow his lead.

invest in the spiritual disciplines of prayer, Bible study and worship.

serve with the gifts he's given us.

draw on his power.

and listen to his testimony.

Eternal Life

Eternal life is not just living forever, it's living forever with God as members of his family, in deep communion with him as we mature into the fullness of all he intends for us to become.

We embrace eternal life by living with an eternal perspective: God is with us forever, the new life we now possess will never end and the hardships we suffer in this life are not worth comparing to all the good things God has prepared for us to enjoy throughout all eternity.

*   *   *

Each of the salvation gifts is uniquely embraced and some require effort on our part to fulfill. Those who are serious about embracing the gifts will need help that is beyond the scope of this book (or any book) to provide, because embracing the gifts does not occur through the pages of a book, but within the context of a family. I'll return to this thought in chapter nineteen.

Chapter
17

Just Six Things
(Then the Seventh)

Avoiding Two Common Errors

In chapter thirteen, I noted that blurring the line between the seventh thing and the other six can lead to an error which seriously undermines the entire project. This error occurs when Jesus' effort to purchase the salvation gifts for us is confused with our efforts to embrace the gifts once we've received them.

If our efforts help to purchase salvation, then our need is not as great, the salvation gift package is not as necessary, Jesus' demonstration of love is not as profound and his sacrificial work on the cross is not as essential as the Bible teaches. Furthermore, grace is diminished (because salvation is no longer a free gift but something which we must earn) and the object of faith shifts from Jesus and what he did for us to ourselves and our efforts.

By mistaking Jesus' effort to purchase the salvation gifts with our efforts to embrace them, we cheat ourselves out of the joy and peace that rightly flow from a correct understanding of the sufficiency of God's salvation, we diminish our appreciation for the depths of his love and we undermine our ability to live in gratitude for all God has done for us.

So let's be clear: Salvation was purchased for us by Jesus' effort alone and offered to us as a free gift which is not and cannot be deserved, earned or paid back. Once in our possession, some of the salvation gifts require our efforts (and the ongoing efforts of the Holy Spirit) to fulfill the purpose for which they were given.

Confusing Jesus' effort to purchase salvation for us with our efforts to embrace the salvation gifts is a serious error and one we should definitely seek to avoid—but not by neglecting the seventh thing.

This is the second of two common errors: Failure to recognize that embracing the salvation gifts requires our effort. Becoming God's ambassadors will require hard work, discipline and study. Growing up to be mature men and women of God will require an investment in the spiritual disciplines of prayer, bible study and worship (among others). It's good work to be sure and it's often joyous, but it takes effort, and we are called to it. Those who fail to answer this call are not likely to mature as God intends.

In summary, there are two common errors we want to avoid in relationship to the seventh thing: The first is confusing our efforts to embrace the salvation gifts with Jesus' effort to purchase them for us. The second is to fail to recognize that the gifts—purchased for us by Jesus' effort alone—require our efforts to fulfill.

Chapter

18

Salvation's Prayer

Having read up to this point, you should have a basic understanding of the seven essentials of salvation: Our need for it, what it consists of, why God provides it, what it cost him to provide it, what it costs us to receive it, and how it is received and embraced.

The following is a prayer for salvation which is informed by salvation's seven things. Those for whom this book has served as an introduction to salvation are invited to express their faith in Jesus (and thus enter into salvation) by means of this prayer. If you would like to do so, read the prayer through once (so that you know what it says) and then read through it again, this time offering it as a prayer to God.

Jesus,

The 1st Thing: I know that, apart from you, I am lost in rebellion and sinfulness, without hope and headed for an eternity outside of your love, joy and peace.

The 3rd Thing: But, I have learned that out of your great love, mercy and kindness for me,

The 4th Thing: you entered into humanity to represent me, suffer for my sinfulness and purchase, at great expense,

The 2nd Thing: a wonderful and complete and generous salvation,

The 5th Thing: which you freely and graciously offer to me as a gift.

The 6th Thing: I do not want to miss out on your generosity and so I come to you now in faith that I might receive every blessing you offer. I confess my sinfulness and acknowledge my need for forgiveness. I invite you into my heart—into the very core of my being—to be changed as you see fit. I fully consent to your generous offer of adoption and spiritual rebirth into your family. I invite you into my life to be at home within me through the presence of your Holy Spirit. I surrender myself—my whole self—to your will and to your care.

The 7th Thing: Grant that I may now live by faith, enjoying the benefits of the salvation you have given me, embracing all you have done for me and looking forward to its completion. Lead me, keep me and grow me by the power of your Holy Spirit, deepening my faith and producing in me more and more of your love, joy, peace and goodness. Reveal to me how I might serve your kingdom and your people. Connect me to others who will teach me about you and encourage me to walk with you and grow in relationship to you.

Thank you. Amen.

Those who sincerely pray the above have properly placed

and appropriately expressed faith in the one who promises to save all who do so. If you have done so, you have been forgiven, justified, adopted, reborn and have received the Holy Spirit. You now possess and can forever enjoy all the rights and privileges that come with being a member of God's family.

Chapter

19

Next Steps

In baseball, the very best players are sometimes referred to as "five tool players", meaning that they have all five of the most important baseball abilities. Five tool players are able to hit for high average, hit with power, field their position with consummate skill, throw accurately with velocity and run with great speed. Think Willie Mays.

Imagine that you have the one time ability to bestow the five baseball tools upon anyone of your choosing and let's say you decide to give these gifts to a neighborhood boy who has a consuming passion for baseball, but only modest ability.

The baseball gifts, freely given, will take effort on the part of the boy to fulfill. Developing the gifts to their potential will require countless hours in the batting cage, the gym and on the diamond. But no matter how hard he works, all his effort and skill will come to nothing apart from a team.

Baseball is a team sport and no one can be a baseball player without a team. You can be a sprinter or a long distance runner or a shot putter without a team, but you can't be a baseball player without a team.

It is the same with salvation. For while we approach Jesus for salvation as individuals, we are adopted and reborn into a family. The life God calls us to embrace is communal in nature. Salvation is a team sport. And those who are serious about embracing the salvation gifts will need to become a part of a team committed to embracing the salvation gifts. This means becoming a part of a local congregation.

Within a local congregation, you'll...

• find people who are farther along the path of spiritual maturity than you are: People who can walk beside you, become your mentors and help you grow in faith and understanding.

• learn the nuts and bolts of what it means to grow up into the person Jesus desires you to become.

• receive blessings from family members who God has uniquely gifted to help and encourage you.

• discover the unique ways God has gifted you to help and encourage others.

• learn how to read and study the Bible

• discover how to worship

• learn to love people who are difficult to love.

Some who read these words will have had a bad experience with a congregation or pastor. I understand. Every group has its bad apples and there are certainly some bad apples out there. And every congregation will have some people who are immature, uncommitted and/or just downright unpleasant. Your goal should not be to find a church filled with perfect people, but rather a church where the core leadership are healthy and devoted to embracing the fullness of life the salvation gifts make possible. Within this group you'll find a mentor who can help you grow and mature into the person God desires you to be.

* * *

Finding the right congregation can be a challenge, but the following steps should help you get started:

First, pray. God knows your needs and can get you to the right place.

Second, search online for Christian churches in your community. Visit their websites and look at their "what we believe" statements. Do they sound like a congregation that's serious about embracing the truth of the Bible and about becoming who God wants them to be?

Third, visit. Go to a Sunday service. Does the pastor preach from the Bible? Check out their bulletin to see what opportunities exist for Bible study and service.

Fourth, talk with the pastor(s). Explain that you're looking for a place that can help you mature into the person God is calling you to become. Ask the pastor a question or two about salvation to see if they're committed to biblical truth. (See the appendix for a list of potential questions.)

Fifth, give it some time. Discovering that a congregation is right for you might take a while. Don't move on too hastily. Remember, you've not looking for perfection.

Sixth, once you've found a good fit, settle in. Attend regularly. Attach yourself to a Bible study. Find a mentor. Look for a way to serve the community. Continue to pray, knowing that the one who died to purchase salvation for you is committed to overseeing your growth.

* * *

This is the bottom line: All who are saved, are saved into the family of God, and it is within this family that God intends for us to experience and embrace the new life he has given. If you have trusted in Jesus for salvation, you need to be a part of a congregation that is committed to embracing the salvation gifts. And if you have yet to put your faith in Jesus, there is no better place for you to continue learning about the salvation God has made available to you than within a congregation that is committed to biblical truth.

Chapter

20

Concluding Thoughts/Personal Remarks

Having read thus far, you should now have a foundational knowledge of salvation's six things: Our need for it, what it consists of, why God provides it, what it cost him to provide it, what it costs us to receive it, and how it's received. Such knowledge requires a response, and I urge you, if you haven't already done so, to invite Jesus into your heart, into the core of your being, so that you might come to possess and enjoy the fullness of the salvation Jesus died to purchase for you.

As I noted in the preface, I was originally motivated to write this book out of concern that, for a variety of reasons, I hadn't adequately communicated the essentials of salvation to the young people in my care. The bottom line is that I don't want anyone to miss out on the opportunity to enjoy the salvation God has prepared.

Life can be hard and we are not intended to go through it alone. During difficult times in my life, I've had occasion to wonder how anyone gets by without Jesus. As I continue to walk in faith, my understanding of my need apart from God, the riches of his salvation and love, the extent of his sacrifice, the generosity of his grace and the necessity of trusting in him continues to deepen. As it does so, I am more and more grateful for all Jesus has done for me, and I am more and more concerned for those who don't know Jesus and the salvation he offers.

So if you have questions, seek answers. Ask God to lead

you into the truth. If you have doubts, take them to God.

If you've had a bad experience in a church, seek a better experience. Search out a place of health. Find someone, a pastor, perhaps, who can mentor you.

Just don't miss out. The salvation gift package is intended to be received, embraced, enjoyed, lived, celebrated and fulfilled. It is the essence of life itself. Don't miss out on the life God wants to give you.

Appendix

Referenced in chapter six: The Trinity

The nature of the Trinity may not be fully understandable for human beings, but Jesus' role in salvation cannot be understood without some familiarity with it. Those who wish to explore the nature of God at a deeper level are encouraged to read James White's book, *The Forgotten Trinity*. I also recommend R. C. Sproul's book, *What Is the Trinity?* Please note that the later is not for beginners.

Referenced in chapter eleven: Evidence for God's existence

Many excellent resources are available for those who wish to explore the evidence for God's existence. Lee Strobel's, *The Case For a Creator*, is a great place to start because most chapters feature a different expert and thus serve as an introduction to each expert's work.

I highly recommend all of Lee Strobel's books to you, particularly *The Case For Christ* and *The Case For Faith*.

Referenced in chapter nineteen: Questions for Pastors

If you're finding it difficult to determine whether the congregation you're attending is committed to biblical truth, it may be helpful to set up a meeting with the pastor so that you can seek direct answers to your questions. Your questions could include the following:

Q: In your understanding of the Bible, does everyone need salvation? (The answer you're looking for is an unqualified "yes".)

Q: What purpose did Jesus' death on the cross serve? (Because of the complexity of this subject, the answer could take many forms, but a pastor should at least mention something about Jesus' death paying the penalty for our sins.)

Q: In your understanding of the Bible, is salvation offered as a free gift or does it have to be earned? (Salvation is offered to us as a free gift.)

Q: What does it mean to be saved by grace? (It means that salvation is offered to us as a free gift. It means that we're saved by a gracious act of God and not by our own efforts.)

Q: What is the essence of salvation? (Salvation includes forgiveness, justification, adoption, rebirth, the receiving of the Holy Spirit and eternal life. Don't worry if the pastor doesn't mention all of the above.)

Q: How does someone receive salvation? (Here again, there are a wide variety of possible responses: A person receives salvation when they trust Jesus with their lives, when they invite Jesus into their hearts, when they surrender their lives to Jesus (or to Christ), when they put their faith in Jesus, etc.)

Q: How can you and this congregation help me to grow and mature in my faith? (Here you're looking for opportunities for discipleship and service.)

You should not expect a pastor to answer your questions using the exact language or phraseology above, but you should expect answers which are consistent with what the Bible teaches.

Acknowledgments

This book is dedicated to my wife, Melinda, who has been and remains God's greatest blessing to me, but I would be remiss if I didn't also acknowledge and thank the many others who have had a significant influence on my life.

I grew up attending the First Presbyterian Church of Concord (California) and benefitted greatly from their children's, youth and young adult ministries. The high school ministry at FPCC was particularly strong under the leadership of Youth Pastor Dave Wilkinson (more on Dave in a moment), High School/College Choir Director Jerry Smith and a cadre of college-aged leaders who were serious about their faith: Scott Mitchell, Chris Williams, Dan Macke, Diane Branscum, Chris MacDonald and Robin Bigones. To all of you (and to the congregation who supported their ministry), thank you for caring. You were my role models and you can't possibly know how important you were to me.

My spiritual journey was largely shaped by two men: Dave Wilkinson (mentioned above) and Dan Vraa. Both modeled for me a life committed to Jesus and an appreciation for and dedication to his Word. Apart from their mentorship, I'd be a very different person, and I am blessed to count them as friends.

A year after graduating high school, I became a youth ministry volunteer with the FPCC high school group. After several years, I left for my first venture into professional ministry at the Ygnacio Valley and Clayton Valley Presbyterian churches (both of Concord)—two small congregations which combined resources to hire me as their part-time Director of Youth Ministry. It was during this time that I met Dan Vraa (who became the pastor at the Ygnacio Valley congregation during my tenure there) and we quickly became friends and confidants.

After seven years with the YVPC and CVPC churches, I returned to FPCC for a couple of years, serving as their Director of Youth and Family Ministries, before settling in at the John Knox Presbyterian Church of Dublin (California), where I've served for the better part of two decades.

I owe so much to each of these congregations, but it's the youth themselves to whom I'm most indebted. Thank you for laughing at my jokes, listening (sometimes) to my lessons and, most of all, for allowing me to share in your lives.

While the majority of my relationships can be chronicled in association with the congregations I've served, many fall outside this framework. In addition to the above, I offer my sincere thanks...

to my sister, who has been an encouragement and confidant for many decades.

to my friends, Brad Paulson and Scott McVitte, with whom I first discovered the joy of writing, not for a teacher or a grade, but for my peers.

to my counselors: Don Paulsen, Ray Campton and Helena Hershel. The combination of your art, science, craft and care nurtured me through difficult times and helped to lay a foundation suitable for flourishing.

to Carol Wilkinson, who is simply the most gracious person I know.

to my friends and family who helped edit and provide feedback for this book: Dan Vraa, Dave Wilkinson, Roger and

Jody Dill, Melinda Byrne and especially Beth Byrne (also known as Mom).

Thank you all, and may you discover and enjoy God's richest blessings...